Athol Williams is a poet and social philosopher from Cape Town. He has published two volumes of poetry (under the pseudonym AE Ballakisten) and his poems have been published in anthologies and literary journals in the UK, USA, and South Africa. He has been invited to read his poems at literary events at home and abroad, including a reading at the Sackler Museum at Harvard. He has written two children's books, including the popular *Oaky and the Sun*, and is the founder of READ TO RISE, an international NGO that promotes social change through literacy. He holds five degrees: from Harvard (where he was a Mason Fellow and a Littauer Fellow), Massachusetts Institute of Technology, London School of Economics and Political Science, London Business School, and Wits, and is currently a political philosophy student at Oxford University.

This is his first poetry collection with **The Onslaught Press** but he contributed two poems to Onslaught's *for the children of Gaza* in 2014.

also by Athol Williams

Poetry (as AE Ballakisten):

Heap of Stones (Theart Press, 2009)
Talking to a Tree (Theart Press, 2011)

Children's Books:

Oaky and the Sun (Theart Press, 2013)
Oaky the Happy Tree (Theart Press, 2015)

other poetry collections published by The Onslaught Press

Waslap (2015)
Rethabile Masilo

Aistear Anama (2014)
Tadhg Ó Caoinleáin

for the children of Gaza (2014)
edited by Mathew Staunton & Rethabile Masilo

Poison Trees (2014)
Philippe Saltel & Mathew Staunton

Bumper Cars

Athol Williams

The Onslaught Press

Published in Oxford by **The Onslaught Press**
11 Ridley Road, OX4 2QJ
August, 2015

ISBN-13 978-0-9927238-7-3

Edited by Mathew Staunton & Rethabile Masilo
Typeset in Le Monde Livre & Le Monde Sans,
designed, & edited by **Mathew Staunton**
Printed by Lightning Source

Acknowledgements

'Fathers' and 'After Killing a Baby Lizard' were published
in *New Contrast* (South Africa)

'Bumper Cars', 'Sent for Psychiatric Assessment' & 'A Sunday Hanging'
were published in *Clare Market Review* (UK)

'We Rise' appeared in the anthology,
for the children of Gaza published by The Onslaught Press (UK)

'If Only It Was That Easy', 'Garden of Defiance', 'where to start'
& a version of 'Kant Playing Chess' appeared in the anthology
here, without: questions for a foreigner published by BBP Gallerie (USA)

'Beggars', 'Uncle John' & 'World Peace' first appeared in
Talking to a Tree published by Theart Press (South Africa)

'Steel Cage' appeared in the movie *Anna & Modern Day Slavery*
produced by Mayan Films (UK)

PERSON TO PERSON

PEOPLE TO PEOPLE

HUMANITY TO HUMANITY

Person to Person

Photograph

They were drawn to the life-sized black
and white photograph hanging on the vast white
wall in the hazy room of light and smoke
that erased everything except this photograph
of a shack—a scrum of bent metal, bits of wire
and plastic fashioned to make a place after many
lifetimes of placelessness. It had a flat roof
with a brick at each corner to pull in the tug of war
with the Cape winds. It had no eyes, only a wide,
open mouth in which stood the blackest naked man
that any of the gallery visitors had ever seen. In his
exquisite form they saw an abdomen of wildebeest
thundering across open plains, his chest a battle shield,
columns for legs, penis thick with embarrassment and
titillation. His distant face faintly lit with the saddest
small eyes, paraffin lamps in a dark village. Enraptured
in his magnificence and metaphor they stood in silence.
"Remarkable," a voice spoke, but no-one responded.

Then he moved, the man, the man in the photograph,
he moved, blinked, and frowned and tilted his head.
Everyone leapt backwards. "Good god!" the same voice
spoke. "Disgusting," another spoke as they all cringed
and covered their noses as his stench burned like tear gas
in their nostrils. Evil flamed in his eyes. When he took
a step forward, everyone dropped their champagne flutes
and canapés, and dashed through the gallery doors.
The gallery made no sales that evening. I didn't care,
with everyone gone, I locked up and went home early.

A Girl Who Looked Like a Boy

Josh was a boy
who said he was Leelah, a girl.
We all laughed, for we like laughing
at people with struggles
especially when their struggles
reveal our smallness.

Josh tried to be a boy,
a good Christian boy,
but he was Leelah, a girl,
a bad pagan girl
whose parents told him that God
does not make mistakes.

The playground and mall
are places of terrible torment
if you're a teenager
with three heads and fifteen arms
and crawl on your back or
if you're a girl who looks like a boy.

So Leelah lived with her
"parents' disappointment
and the cruelty of loneliness."
She agonised in public
to our embarrassment
and suffered in the darkness of her pillow
with our rejection ringing like church bells
and our jeers stabbing like nails into a cross
as she tried to sleep.

"If you are reading this, it means
that I have committed suicide," she wrote,
her hard resolve and soft flesh no match
for the unforgiving truck as she walked into the
welcome embrace of oncoming highway traffic.

"The human spirit cannot be bent,"
but Leelah's human spirit was broken
by the power of our fear
that demands robotic replication
rather than the beauty of truth.
We taught her to hate herself
by showering her with our hatred;
we punished her for being Black
when we are White, we punished her
for being Muslim when we are Christian,
we punished her for being Jewish
when we are Nazi, we punished her
for being a slave, whose eyes reflect our hatred,
when we are slavemasters. We willed her away
because she was one of 'them' rather than 'us,'
as 'us' always does to 'them.'

By going away
she helped restore order,
returning comfort to our days.
"My death needs to mean something,"
her last words, and it does,
for those awake
do not wear the cloak of order
and comfort born of another's death.

And more are awaking,
as I have awoken,
for our lives must mean more
than her death.

Leelah was a girl who looked like a boy.
All she wanted was to be a girl
who looked like a girl; all she wanted
was for us to be human
who loved like humans.

In memory of Leelah (Joshua) Alcorn
(15 November 1997—28 December 2014)

The Blind That See—Version I

Abel is an old man who carries a gun;
he pretends to be blind,
walking erratically with his white stick
into oncoming traffic;
cars brake violently and swerve
to avoid crashing into this blind, old man.
His hope
is that some fool will stop to help him,
and then he'll take their cellphone, wallet, car
and life, if they get in his way.

Sadly for Abel,
no-one cares enough to stop.

Khiba's Luck

Khiba had prayed for dry weather, but the hatred
in Sihle's eyes, when he opened his, spoke his god's
reply. She had already moved his shoes from the path
of large drops crashing spitefully into a liquid corpse.
Sihle often mocked his size-eight feet in those size-ten
brogues, which she said were "out of fashion and out
of luck." They stared at him unapologetically, "how
were we to know the roof would leak!"

Closer to night than morning, Khiba got dressed;
no food, no kiss, no "good luck," just Sihle's eyes,
like fists in his back, willing him out of their patchwork
shack into the curse that now dripped from his head.
As he wove through the tragic Diepsloot quilt, he felt
his brogues sink deep into the soft orange-red mud
under the weight of his hope and his wife's faithlessness.
He walked gingerly up to the road for the ten-mile
hike to his interview. In his one hand, their 'rainy day'
—the coins filled his fist—in the other, the job ad—
"the ideal candidate will be a clean, mature gentleman."
Old man Khiba was mature alright.

When you see the path to ill-being;
you also see the path to well-being.

Khiba saw no path as he wove back down to their shack,
closer to morning than night, his brogues disappearing
with each heavy step, like he was walking on stumps.
Sihle's things were already stuffed into a bag when
he entered the icy shack, liquid corpses everywhere,
covered with his clothes. Rain poured from both their
clouds. She did not look at him, only his unclean shoes.

His stare reached deep into her mouth to choke the demon before she could speak. She stormed out, wearing her new rainboots, but the rain had already stopped. With his prayers answered, Khiba's face recalled a smile as he sat down to clean his lucky brogues.

Streetclass Diseases

Abeeda's toothless mouth sprays saliva
as she paints a picture of her thirteen years
on Cape Town's streets. He feels her spit in
his face, on his nose, on his lip, arousing
his middleclass concern over streetclass
diseases. At sixty two, she's never been
to a doctor or hospital; he goes twenty times
a year. Distracted by her dark purple
gums, he misses part of her sermon chastising
him for his pagan life of walking past sick
children drowning in ponds and admiring
his large shadow on cave walls and buying
signed first editions of dead poets while
old women starve on Cape Town's streets. She
tells of her walk with her god, her simple
life beneath bridges, clearly boasting
about her immunity to his diseases. He offers
her cash. She scoffs and carries on digging
through the garbage bin, where he found her.

Empty Spaces

I walked into a family's house—
I felt boxed in, my head touched the low ceiling;
it was dark, it had just one small window;
it was cold, it had an earthen floor with no covering;
it had no fridge, no stove, no television;
it had no bathroom, no toilet.

I met the family, and though their house
was empty,
I could feel that this house
was filled
with love.

I walked into another family's house—
I felt small, the rooms were vast;
it was bright, the light blinded me;
it was opulent, excess dripped from every surface;
it had appliances and gadgets and furniture
like a showroom, baths the size of swimming pools,
rooms like cathedrals, gardens like parks.

I met the family, and though their house was empty
(for there is more emptiness
in a mansion than a shack),
I could feel that this house
was filled
with love.

Canterbury Morning

The birds chirped
hurriedly,
as if to sing their songs before
being drowned out by the noise
of cars and buses
and the silent screams
of lonely men.

Thirteen Pieces of Rope

I

Rope,
thick, frayed
with hope,
being tugged
mercilessly.
Fibres,
the colour of desert sand
point to the sea,
to the hills,
to everywhere,
strained
by anger.

II

Severed threads fall
and splash like tears—
squeezed, wrung
from this rope's intertwined history.
Whence the cotton
born into this society
of threads wrapped so tightly?

III

The rope's ancestors
once stood in bright fields,
golden flakes
on tall stems
singing to life.

Fluffy powdery, soft
candly floss, white,
that bounced
with possibility—
baby's shirt,
grandma's throw
or the woven strands of
rope, thick
to one day be frayed.

IV

Why do I care about this rope?
Is it not to blame?
Look, it bears the skin
of men's palms
and the blood of their brows.
It stands between.
What if it were shorter,
the rope?

V

We've flung this rope over trees
and around men's necks
and around little girls' wrists.

VI

I know
as you know
that the frayed threads

are scales on a serpent's
back, and that only one end
of the rope has fangs.
But which end?
Only the men
with fanged piercings know.

VII

We keep struggling
(though some are already yesterday)
and tugging
because this is war
and this is what we do in war
and though the rope frays
and hope fades
we pull
because
there's a rope to be pulled
and gods to be praised.

VIII

I am not afraid
of the cold.
It is the desert that I fear
for that is where men go
to die; to hold onto
either end of life
and pull, in
a tug-of-hope
a tug-of-meaning

a tug-of-dignity,
war,
which splits threads
like hands thrown in the air.
"What are we doing?"
the rope threads ask.

IX

I am standing there,
heels dug deep into the desert
sand, hot on my skin.
I caress the rope, its back,
with my fingertips;
I feel the ridges
twirled along its length;
I feel its roughness.
I have always liked textures
like those found on sofas and rugs,
and warm blankets; the roughness
of a cracked headstone.
But the rope's skin is the texture
of an old tree trunk,
dark, and in pain;
crevices run long
and deep
like scorched, cracked cathedral floors,
rugged and violent
and piercing.

X

I pull
and lean into those behind me
and away from those others.
Then there is only me
and that rope—
thick, frayed,
afraid.
I was pulling
and still I pulled.
All of the me's and I's
pulled, and tugged
and seemed to stare
at that rope
that lay horizontal, erect
like a spear
thrown into abdomens.
Were we pushing in
or pulling out?

XI

I moved from high to low
from hard to soft—
is that not the dream,
movement?
More to the east,
more to the west,
less in the middle
on this great ball of rope,
cotton threads and twine,

27

fibre
spun
and spinning
in nothingness.
Why do we pull on this part of it?

I am tired.

XII

There should be a song
perhaps sung by Elton John,
an apology—
Mohammed Ali's rope-a-dope,
Michael Schumacher crashed on a slope.

XIII

But all there is,
is the will of man
at the end of a rope—
thick, frayed,
that rope, in silence,
until it gives up its struggle
to end ours.

Stomach Virus

I vomited
all over the front of my new suit
as I watched him
die, that man, hated to death
because he walked on God's green earth
across a synthetic line
manufactured by lies
that awake Satan from his afternoon nap
to hasten every man's death. This man,
from a circle called 'them'
trapped like a stomach virus in a circle called 'us.'

'Us' always chooses to kill 'them,' and so
with sticks and metal rods and rocks,
'us' slowly reshaped his spirit
and rewrote Ubuntu—
"People are *dead* people
through other *dead* people."

This small group of Diepsloot men,
standing in an open wound,
on a vast field, littered with garbage
and fallen hope, like brothers
gathered for a choir rehearsal,
but fallen for the truth of priests
like politicians, like Hollywood writers
about good, evil, ally, enemy,
about who *we* are
and who *they* are:
Who are they, if not us?

He tried to stand,
but someone kicked him in the chest,
straight back he fell into a pool of stagnant pus;
he got onto his knees
but a pole in the back thrust him forward onto his face;
Nkosi Sikelel' iAfrika
I wonder if he heard the hymn, if he
felt the warmth of the African afternoon sun, if
he felt his mother's heart beat in his chest
like those moments before he came to the light
that led to this darkness.

A rock to the ribs to silence the song
of life refusing to be still.
Then on his back, eyes to heaven,
but seeing Satan,
he held up his left leg to block the thieves
who were gnawing at his spirit with their blows.
Metal rod to his shin,
but not even a wince—an overdose
of pain makes us immune to pain, like an overdose of lies
makes us believers, immune to truth. The crowd gathered
to see Jesus being crucified;
some cheered the soldiers,
some shrieked, but no-one cried, no-one
ran to cover his brokenness with their bodies.

A righteous man lifted a rock high above his head
and whipped it into the man's chest—
Amen to his muted prayers.
Blow after blow, they took it in turns,
as though in a rehearsed tribal dance,

the natural rhythm of things.
A man in the crowd filmed with his cellphone;
a young man stood right in front, soccer ball in hand,
taking a break from his game, *he* winces,
in delight. What do you see young man?
What is it that delights you so?

And then hatred personified, and mutated
into something that looks like me
and thinks like me, and acts like me
to raise a thick pipe high into the baby blue sky
and smack it repeatedly into the man's face—once:
In the name of the father
a second time:
In the name of the son
and a third time:
In the name of my unholy spirit
and then Farai Kujirichita
the 26-year-old Zimbabwean,
who came here in hope,
was dead,
forsaken.

They all left,
the man with the pipe,
and the man with the rod,
and the rock throwers,
and the men who kicked
and the men who laughed
and the men who go to church every Sunday
and march to demand
respect for life and relief from suffering.

They all went home
to their wives,
kissed their children,
sat down for a hot meal
and talked about sports with friends
like imperialist heroes
after a good day of
"upholding freedom."

It must have been a stomach virus;
vomit poured uncontrollably
down my chin,
onto my new suit,

as I stood there,
like a gravestone,
watching humanity wither.

Fathers

How were we to live without our fathers,

absent fathers, invisible fathers,
negligent fathers, fathers who failed
to escape the ash that blesses all
who stand beneath clouds, faces upturned,
in search of the dignity that comes
with taking home a half-loaf of bread?

How were we to know that these fathers,
angry fathers, depleted fathers,
tired fathers, would never return
to remove their shadow from the sun?

Freedom rumbles in our empty hands,
frightened hands, our fathers' gift to us.

How are we supposed to live as fathers?

Beggars

I begged there every day,
at the same traffic light,
corner of Rivonia Rd and Outspan Rd,
for scraps,
for coins,
for mercy,
from those in BMWs and Jaguars and Audis
with a crumpled cardboard sign that read:
PLEASE HELP. NO FOOD. NO JOB.

I'd be on bended knees
that struck the earth,
cushioned by the hard, jagged asphalt;
my head bowed low,
my face pitiful.
I'd imitate the queen,
and wave the royal beggar wave
to draw attention
like an idiot
as fumes from five-litre engines
filled my empty stomach.
The crumpled cardboard sign in my heart read:
PLEASE HELP. NO HOPE. NO DIGNITY,
for I had dissolved a long time ago.

The faces in the cars would ignore me,
awkwardly, they'd turn away,
away from me,
away from their shame
and wave a dismissive hand,
"Fuck off,
go get a job!"

I'd been offered a job
but I didn't want it;
I'd rather stand there.
The faces were right,
I should fuck off
because I didn't have to be there.
So I would be a beggar
and be ignored
and be sworn at
and get saliva-soaked leftover sandwiches
or a cigarette butt
or pneumonia.

Then one day I took that job,
abandoned my corner
to the relief of the faces
in the BMWs and Jaguars and Audis.

But I still see those faces,
only now they don't ignore me;
waving, pleading, bowing, bending,
begging,
only now it's not me.
*"Please don't take our things,
please don't hurt us,"*
they beg.

We're actually all the same,
beggars;
it just depends on who holds the power
to grant wishes,
and who's on their knees.
"Fuck off," I say, cocking my gun,
"this is my job!"

A Sunday Hanging

"From the moment we are born, we start
to forget," the blaspheming thief proclaimed,
as the thick rope was placed over his despicable head.
"We start to forget what our tongues have known for
millennia. We start to forget the geometry of our whole,
the algebra of our truth." He had been caught with an
ancient drawing stolen from the home of a dying priest,
and accused of hurrying the priest's death. "As our mothers'
heartbeats grow silent in our chests, we forget our footsteps
in a golden time, an age of walking-with: man, rhinoceros,
tree, the Great Flame," as the rope was tightened in place.

"We are born chanting the psalms of the angels but silenced,
our mouths crammed with worship that chokes the wisdom
we know, for angel voices are like pinpricks to pagan ears.
We are wrapped with layers that add to our vocabulary but
renders us mute. Our seeing eyes like large windows
negligently left open for progress to sneak in by day and
escape with our souls. We celebrate walking apart, synthetic
rains on barren lands, cracked ocean floors that drain
our spirits of abundance. We become more man but less
human, more like our fathers and less like ourselves."
The crowd jeered and spat at him. "And so, to gaze

upon man-before-man, the still-cocooned caterpillar,
bearing heart-shaped wings of a miracle on its back,
before it unfurls and blooms, is to gaze upon truth,
upon beauty, to know the most spiritually pure state of man.
Da Vinci knew, he remembered, and by his studies in ink
and chalk, left a reminder, lest our memories, our humanity,
fail completely." Then justice silenced him,
and everyone went back to church.

Steel Cage

Am I trapped?
They've locked me
in a steel cage. Unseen, I crouch
in my smallness.

Why is steel so cold and so grey,
and so hard? Why does it echo
so loud when shame beats against
my ribcage, a steel door slamming
eternally into its steel frame? This

is not the first steel cage and mine
is not the first freedom stolen. All
around, since birth, we are locked
in steel cages to contain our dreams,
to erase from memory the shape of
                                our freedom.

Who are they, these thieves? They
are the mothers who buy dresses
made with my bleeding hands; the
family who eats dinner of seafood
and meat that hold my soul; young
man who proposes to his lover with
a diamond that crushed my back;
boys' night out that violates and
pours acid into the wounds of my
dancing sisters. Your morning fruit,
your evening dinner, your child's
first toy, the warm clothing you wear,
these are my tormenters. I crouch
caged in your shops, your fields, your

building sites and have my heart
ripped out behind the curtains of the
houses of your ordinary streets, where
good men find Satan, and good families
pound out prayers louder and louder
to block out the screams of my anguish.

Used and discarded I am. I look with
horror at my reflection, I see the
rotting beast that I have become.
They do not see my humanity, they
do not see a person, they see a savage,
an alien, an insect that little boys
torture, pulling off its legs and wings
one by one, for amusement.

Can we steal
a human? Can a person's spirit be stolen,
trapped, contained, caged? Only that
which can be owned can be stolen, and
there is no human who can be owned. They
are fools! For the human spirit cannot be
contained. The spirit does not forget the
shape of freedom, it *is* the shape of
freedom. Let it be known that while we
have life, we have hope, and so I straighten
my twisted, bent body and stand upright, and push
aside this cage. I am free! I am free! He, who
chips at the spirit of another, erodes his own
spirit. *They* are the caged, *I* am the free. The
thieves are crouched in the steel cages of
their ignorance and their gluttony, and their
self-righteousness, not I.

The flame that rises within me
                              melts the shadows,
and casts out the darkness, and
                              raises my eyes to truth,
and so I know, like we all know, like
they know, that I cannot be owned,
cannot be stolen.

                    My spirit stands proudly,
stands free. The human spirit cannot be
contained; it does not forget the shape
of freedom. I stand outside the steel cage,
seen, unstolen, free.

Called

Along the road back to Cape Town,
I stopped in Swellendam
where I saw a flock of sheep
grazing; a dog's sharp bark
startled them all, instantly
causing some to pee.

I stopped at a church
in Montagu, where we were
called to be like sheep.
I tried hard not to pee when
the preacher startled me
with his sharp words.
In the town I noticed
that brown sheep lived in dirty little houses
while the white sheep occupied estates.

At Robertson I picked up a hitchhiker,
a policeman, in full uniform, with badge
and gun and bulletproof vest, called
to protect the interests of distant others.
He had no transport to get to work.
We spoke about pride and dignity,
and freedom, and how sheep
have none of these.

In Cape Town I met a Congolese
man who was tending cars,
all lined up obediently along
the side of the road. He had
his father's hands he said,
as we shook. He told me

he felt called to South Africa
to search for work, a search
that we both knew
would end bloody,
with much bleating.

In a trance I followed others
back down the mountain
and got home to write this text
which I felt called to do.
I sat in silence, wondering about my
journey, and all those callings,
when the neighbour's dog barked
causing me to wet myself.

People to People

Chocolate Tin

In a Tulbagh antique store
I find a chocolate tin.
I lift the misshapen lid;
nothing inside but the
echo of its squeaking
arthritic hinges. I hold
the open tin to my ear
like a rusty seashell,
the size of a postcard.
Speak tin, I whisper,
waiting, hoping to hear
the voice of the boy
who held this tin in 1940.

Greetings from South Africa,
the tin spoke to him as he crouched
in fear somewhere distant, fighting
another's war as all wars are.
We rely on you and are grateful
the then-shiny tin with its payload
of Christmas chocolates beamed.
Chocolates for my blood, he
probably muttered drawing the ire
of fellow boys sent there as sacrifice
to the ego of the man-god, but
hoping to defer the hour of their
offering. Did the tin's gold-plated,
embossed portrait of the President,
Jan Smuts, give him any comfort?
The stern president, with his gruff
voice saying, *fight for South Africa
son, fight for humanity, for freedom.*

To Russell the inside lid reads in an
awkward hand, probably by a kind
middle-aged lady who sat in Pretoria,
a volunteer with the *South African
Gifts and Comforts Committee*
perhaps, dreaming of love, of
honour and bravery, and the mystical
men travelled to distant deathlands
who could manufacture these.
Smile Russell she would breathe
while packing the tin with desire,
*we are thinking of you, come home
soon, here are chocolates.*
Chocolates! Russell would exclaim,
fucking chocolates for my blood?
It brought no comfort as gunshots
spat everywhere, and Russell shot
that boy, and killed this boy, and
wounded that other boy, and hid
there and ducked here, with the tin
in his breast pocket when he was
killed, leaving dark brown marks
either side of Smuts' head, tracks
of the tears of his soul falling
to earth or his spirit's footsteps,
rising to heaven.

I can't tell if the marks
are chocolate or blood.

I hear nothing in the tin,
so remove it from my ear,
looking around embarrassed,
hoping no-one has seen me
standing with a World War II
Christmas chocolate tin
to my ear. I return it to the table
piled high with junk, as war
renders the spirits of men.

After Killing a Baby Lizard

It was my fear
of you
that showered poison
upon your head.

I heard you scream,
a chorus of shrieks
that reverberated violently
around my emptiness.

I watched
in disgust
as you wriggled—bending, twisting, flipping—
trying to clear your world of my evil.

For a moment you looked as though you were having fun,
playfully wriggling
as though, with a tiny toy.
"I've done good," I lied to myself.

Invading soldiers know my lie;
I wonder
how many
know my disgust.

Uncle John

They fought against Midian, as the Lord commanded Moses, and killed every man.
Moses said, "Now kill all the boys. And kill every woman ..." Numbers 31

"We have always been killing each other,"
Uncle John replied, calmly, matter-of-factly
with a hint of "don't come here to preach
your new-age leftist nave shit." *Always?*
"Khoikhoi killing San,
Vikings killing Irish,
Romans killing English,
English killing Boers." *But thou shalt*
not kill, Uncle John, "Germans
killing Polish,
Japanese killing Chinese,
Americans killing Iraqis." *But thou shalt*
not kill, Uncle John. "Israelites
killing Midianites!" he continued, measured
another length of wood, sawed and
nailed to craft a rectangular wooden box
in which a boy would take his place
alongside mankind to fulfil his destiny.
"We have always been killing each other,
so who are you
to say that we should stop
when it is what we have always been doing,
led by kings, by popes, by God!"

Uncle John was clearly possessed by the devil,
so I killed him.

If Only It Was That Easy

A young woman was my neighbour
on the flight from Cape Town to Johannesburg—
the drudgery of my weekly ritual,
like the drudgery
of removing discarded lives from rubble,
and rubble from buildings,
and buildings from the land,
and the land from people,
and people from memory.

I noticed her alabaster skin and emerald eyes,
and her attentive marble breasts under a grey
college sweater. She caught me leering once
or twice, but I had no shame, I was drawn to them
like to freedom.

I sat propped in my cheap seat, distracted
by the thought of the chasm between desire
and courage.
Why do we not just reach out to touch
our dreams?
I reached out ...

... to take the tray of dinner being served.
My neighbour grumbled loudly, and complained
to the flight attendant that her breadrolls were stale.
That's just the way they are, we like them firm,
I sniggered to myself, having eaten these rubber turds
many, many times.
But then the attendant brought her a pair
of fresh rolls. 'Marble breasts' accepted them
like a gold medal. I felt the old fool.

We've got to take what we want, I thought.
I wonder if Palestinians have tried this.

"Excuse me miss," I raised my hand in the direction
of the flight attendant, "My rolls are also stale,
could I please also get a fresh pair." But she reminded me
on which side of the wall I sat, "Sorry sir" she spat,
"we are all out!"
Fuck that, I thought,
and I reached, groping, across to my neighbour
who turned, and with biblical venom,
slapped me.

So I just sat there,
pent up,
propped up,
eating my turd rolls.

Garden of Defiance

*My heart dresses in black
and dances.*
                    Mary Oliver

It wasn't big at all, her garden—its length
as tall as a grown man, a toddler's height
its breadth; about the size of the kitchen
table where they all once sat. A grassy
patch outside her door lying prostrate
over sodden sand, soaked deep green
with pictures and words that slip away
so easily, heavily. The grass grows
defiantly in loose sand, naked
of nutrients, yet perfectly manicured
like those fake football fields where
the others play, or her 'landing strip' which
he had liked. From the air an emerald
blot on a perfect grey canvas in a gallery
of vacant rooms like abandoned wombs.

She walked there daily, her feet naked
to the soft grass wagging like happy
tongues under her soles and fingers
waving in the breeze as though in song
at church. The tongues sang to her, chanted,
sometimes hymns like *Amazing Grace*.
It was her ritual, like a cleansing, in which
she walked the length slowly, a shuffling
pace, and then the breadth of a toddler's
height, and then over and over again
making smaller and smaller rectangles
until she reached the centre of the garden;
stopping only to genuflect and pick up
a piece of shrapnel or a chunk of the
neighbourhood or pamphlets that rained
from heaven instructing her to evacuate
her home; that home
surrounded by landfills of disposable people.

She knows that the land is not hers
and the garden is not hers
and that one day it will be taken
as all things are taken by those
chosen to take.

She is young, and old,
a woman, a stone, and something else,
but she's not a stranger, not lost.
She hates, and loves;
she never looks up, afraid
that God might see her.

Sometimes when the grass reached up
from the earth like daggers, middle
fingers, tongues wagging tarred words,
she would sit down, lean on her
left hand, and with her right she'd draw
from her grease-brown apron pocket
a small pair of nail scissors; she'd take
the green fingers in hers, and then carnage—
fingers are cut at the first digit spraying
their peaceful objection everywhere;
green tongues are silenced, their songs
muted by the pincering strategy of her
scissor blades. And so stillness ...
and silence. She listens
for her husband's snoring
and her daughter's giggles
but all she hears is jetfighters
roaring overhead in defeat,
and sniper bullets ricochet
off hardened hearts.

The Only Way

Mine is the only way
My holy book says so
So I must be right

Your holy book says
That yours is the only way
So you must be right

Their holy book says
That theirs is the only way
So they must be right

For holy books don't lie

But we all can't be right
Which is why we must fight
Defying all our holy books

Proving that none of us are right
And none of ours is the only way

where to start

it is an occupation
we cannot be blind
to the occupation
we've got to talk about
the occupation
and start stating our case
from the occupation
which creates settlers
and indigenous
those who belong
and those who must go
those who came
and those who were here
those who own
and those who stole
we must start our discussion
with the occupation
we can't solve anything
without acknowledging the occupation
it all starts with the occupation

it's the terrorists, the bombers,
our security, our state, so we need the wall
we've got to start with our right to exist
and our security,
our security of state
and the security of our homes
and the security of our faith
and the dangers of our neighbours
who threaten our existence
and our faith
and our livelihoods

and our security
it is for security that we need the wall
and the checkpoints
and the iron dome
and the jetfighters
it starts with the danger
it starts with security

but they were both obviously wrong

neither position was the place the start

for our memories are too short
and our fears too long
and so I held their hands
and we felt the pulse
of our heartbeats
in each other's palms
and we all remembered how to smile

for our dreams are equally long
and our years equally short

Radio News

Sharp, scratchy crackles pierce
from the dusty old boom-box radio
on the bench in his dilapidated workshop
which is failing at the knees but held up by faith.

The radio spews only occasional muffled words
like a forgetful stuttering old toothless man,
(the type seen every day squatting on discarded oil cans,
their eyes dried-up lakes, their faces, desert maps,
mumbling nothings to no-one in particular,
still trying to rid their souls of circling memories)
while he replaces black greasy metal parts of a tired
car engine that spews only occasional horsepower.

He's turned that radio every angle, to get a better signal
and better news. It seems some place called *Heaven*
(or *Hairmen*?) has experienced two strikes from the sky,
killing two people. "Lightning", he says to himself,
shaking his head, testing the spark plugs for fire.
What luck that the two killed were terrorists.
The sputtering radio voice proclaims ...
that's twenty two strikes this year ...
making him chuckle—"seems that unlucky place
should be named *Hell* not *Heaven*." The smile
feels good on his face ... it's been a while.

With the engine ready
he fills the car with his bodyweight
in dynamite, and heads out
for his morning delivery.
All afternoon the radio crackles
shredded sentences,
words scattered like shrapnel.

Unless

Thou shalt not kill
Unless you're afraid
Or made uncomfortable
By the smell of their skin
Or the look of their hair
Or the clothes that they wear
Or the prayers that they pray
Or the hatred they have
For the wrong that you did
Taking the oil that they have
Or the land that they own
Or the leader they follow
Or the freedom they live
Or the love that they hold

Thou shalt not kill
Unless it is hidden
Or made sweet with your words
Or made just with your theory

Thou shalt not kill
Unless the party of five
Give their nod
Or the party of one
Assumes the role of god
For the man with the gun
Is god to the girl on her knees

Thou shalt not kill
Unless
Unless many things
Unless everything

Thou shalt not kill
Is a lie
We can choose
To kill or not
There are no laws
Only our humanity

What a Soldier Learns

I asked him what he had learned,
as the soldier with the record
for the longest tour of duty,
for a people who now
seemed not to remember him,
or the wars. After he drained
his store of Hollywood lessons,
of bravery and survival and honour,
and I drained another beer,
he told me what a soldier learns:
"I have always known
that the food we eat,
shapes our bodies,"
the army veteran said,
"I have come to know
that the deeds we commit,
shape our spirits."
His hands shook uncontrollably,
but I was the one unable to hold
my glass, even the beer seemed
to quiver as he continued:
"Just as bad food has misshapen
my body, my bad deeds have
misshapen my spirit;
and my despicable deeds,
these contort and deform my spirit
so severely
that it weighs heavily on my body,
heavier than the combat gear I carried,
causing my body to cave in
and begin to rot,
till it is not what I've eaten

but what I've *done*
that presents the horror,
that is me,
each time I look in the mirror
to see that my sad, deformed spirit
is visible
in my unrecognizable face.

I have learned,
that the human spirit
is weak, defenceless,
against the despicable
daily chores of war;
that every act of war
hastens suicide
of the soldier's spirit.

During my years of service
to fear, when I listened closely
beneath the voices
of manufactured hatred
toward a manufactured enemy,
I would hear my spirit speak
in a strained, choked whisper:
You cannot kill,
without being killed;
both parties to a killing die.
My spirit was wrong
because I survived,
I thought.
But by this living death,
that only a soldier knows,

that I now live,
I have come to learn
that my spirit was right."
There was nothing to say,
I ordered him a drink,
which brought a smile.

What Shall I Eat?

I tried to quieten the stampede
of my hunger with a serving of
democracy, but the rattle of chains
deep in the dark of my gut only
magnified, as hope, and strength,
faded. It did not fill me. It had
no nutrients, not even any flavour.

I stare bleakly, as the hungry do,
at a blank menu—
I could pay with my freedom,
to get some daily black bread
that will brighten the dungeons
and tame the beasts, make melodic
the rattling. Or have another
serving of their democracy, freely
choosing starvation.

The waitress, like death,
taps her foot impatiently,
waiting for my vote ...

Escaping Extinction

I caught up with the rhino
being chased by armed men,
corrupt men, evil, despicable
parasitic men.

"I am here to save you," I shouted,
over the thumping of hooves
on dry red ground
and the chaos in my chest.
But the rhino just kept on running.
"I am here to save you," I shouted,
louder this time.
"How can you save me,"
the rhino returned
"when you cannot save yourself?"
"I am here to save you," I repeated,
still running at full pace,
the earth rumbling,
clouds of red dust in our wake,
"from what danger?" he asked,
"from these men," I threw back,
"from extinction," with deep caring
and sincerity on my breath.

The rhino slowed his run,
turned his ancient face
with innocent eyes toward me.
He tilted his head with compassion,
"the band of men are not after me,"
he replied, "extinction is not my fate."
I looked back,
there were thousands of armed men,

corrupt men, evil, despicable
parasitic men, millions of blind men.

I drew a sudden deep breath
inhaling my terror, and fearfully
hastened my pace.

Coat of Arms

Heavy in the heavens, a blackened sun
cries death-rays of despair upon the bird
of rising glory with broken wings. One
by one truths fade, every promised word

drips from the scroll, our nation's motto mist
upon a disheartened, perished protea,
and wilted wheat, which drank, could not resist
the poisoned air. We embrace the idea

of voice, while elephant tusks of wisdom
are cracked, our heritage poached, unity
melted into a deformed golden shield, freedom
defeathered, replaced with insanity.

To the gods of hope, faithfully we pray,
"Give tomorrow the hope we lost today."

*In protest against the introduction, in 2011, of the South
African Protection of State Information Bill ('Secrecy Bill')
which limits the public's access to government information
and undermines freedom of speech.*

What Philosophers Say

Humans differ;
difference leads to conflict,
so humans will always be in conflict,
but we are saved—
the state contains conflict through castration,
politics masks conflict through contestation,
ethics pours sugar water on the flames,
and so we become peaceful, patriotic, righteous,
like endless rows of grey concrete blocks,
not living, but better than dead.

Cecil the Lion is Killed

Reporters wrote:
"Cecil the lion *was* killed,"
but they got it wrong.

Every day
Cecil the lion *is* killed—
shot, left to suffer,
beheaded, skinned,
by evil men

as he stands up
to the hatred of the small,
or refuses to bend
to the threats of the fearful,
or fights wannabe masters
who seek to claim his dignity.

Every day
Cecil the lion *is* killed—
shot, left to suffer,
beheaded, skinned,
by evil men

as he learns in school
or walks in the street
or prays in church
or goes to work.

Cecil the lion is everywhere,
every day, he is shot, left to die;
we just don't see him
in the face of the poor,
the aged, the abused,
the vulnerable, the oppressed.

Every day, he is shot, Cecil
the lion, the little girl, the old man,
from the darkness in which we hide
with our cross-bows and killing permits.

Every day
Cecil the lion *is* killed
shot, left to suffer,
beheaded, skinned,
by evil men, me, you.

Humanity to Humanity

Bumper Cars

In Cuckooland, all people drive
in bumper cars—little odd-shaped
fibre-glass cars with thick rubber bands
around the waist, like those we rode
at the fair as kids. Everyone
has the same sized car with identical
power. They go to work or school
or the grocery store in cars of every
possible colour, a kaleidoscope
of dots in Brownian Motion like
looking into a microscope at the
life in a vibrant cell. But there are
no roads, no lanes, no traffic lights,
no stop streets—they drive wherever
they like. And occasionally, when
their cars collide, they wave with
all fingers, not just one, smile
pleasantries, and continue on their way.

Kant Playing Chess

Immanuel Kant was an ethical cosmopolitan in his chess playing;
he believed that the pawns had equal moral value to the bishop;
that the knight and castle were equal to the queen, and that they all
had equal moral value to the king, without restriction of ego or borders;
the blue bishop equal to the red pawn; green queen equal to the white castle.

Kant believed that all pieces had equal moral value and so equal right
to place—on blue and white squares, red and green squares, in fact,
Kant preferred no squares at all.

Kant played chess believing that every piece should be treated as an end,
not as a means to an end; each piece with dignity.

And so Kant lost every chess match that he played, all reluctantly;
and got punched in his grey face, often.

Her Song

She sang sweetly,
a Hebrew song,
the girl born after '67,
wearing a bright green dress
in an underground shelter
grey with despair. Her voice,
like a worker of miracles,
turned blasts to melodies,
thick smoke to light,
and anger to joy that overflowed.
It cast no shadows,
and asked no questions,
it untangled the tangled,
and tore down the walls,
and tunnels and checkpoints
and fears. And sprayed
the sweetest warm honey mist
on everyone in its path.

I did not understand a word of her song,
but my heart knew that it was beautiful;
and like her and all things of beauty,
it needed to be protected and shared.

Sent for Psychiatric Assessment

Strawberries, like red manna, were everywhere.
Voluptuous, inviting heaven-on-earth-red-angel-
heart-shaped bodies of everything lay in abundance.
Oak tree branches hung low with strawberries,
not acorns, dripping with strawberry syrup.
Strawberry birds dashed and darted while in
their nests little strawberries lay in twos or
threes. The sun shone with deep red radiance,
the hills looked succulent and oozed slow
viscous red rivers of sunshine syrup that slithered
into the valley that waited wanting, with lips
agape, undulating tongue, where the president
was a strawberry, men and women were in a state
of strawberryness, all supporting Strawberry United.
All day, everywhere, strawberries, but I could
not touch, I could not taste them, I would not, I
was afraid. Who wants that many strawberries?
What if we wanted prickly pear instead?

The report read, "Just cracked reason leaking some
imagination, a trickle of belief when the mask slips."
I don't care for the report, but I do love strawberries.

World Peace

If I draw a circle around me
and you draw a circle around you,
then I am 'us'
and you are 'them'
and so we use all our strength and skill
and ingenuity and resources to
kill each other.

If we draw a circle
around both of us,
then we are brothers
and there is only 'us.'

Magic

I want to perform some
magic; make a fountain
appear in the desert sand,
make a mountain turn to
nougat; defy gravity by
leaping from tree to tree,
or run faster than the
speed of dreams, or bend
the unbendable, or lift the
unliftable, or perhaps ...
make those frightened men
who kill in vain to rid their
hearts of fear, to stop; to
lift their faces to light,
and to see ... life. Ah magic!

Words

Words dance upon air
that flows over tongues—
breath—
powerful breath
with infinite paths
to come alive
in sound—
a grunt, a curse,
a song to soothe the wounded,
a prayer to lift the soul.

Words, like airstreams,
can lift the spirit's wings
or break them.

Just air
flowing over tongues
that carry the magic of sound
soaked with the power of intention—
words—
that can change the world.

Xenophobia

Seems I'm not alone—the sun rests
but not the beasts at my window.
In fear I relieve my mattress springs
of their roles as pylons, but they creak
with disappointment for they relish
the mosquito bites their sharp edges
offer, sucking deeply into my sleep.
At my fourth floor window are angry,
flailing arms, banging on the glass.
Why have they come?
I did not steal three pounds at Tescos—
check the cameras; I did not insult
John Rawls, all I asked was that he
be quiet for a little while so we could
hear the others, who had more to say—
Krishnamurti, Tagore, perhaps.

I notice that the arms have not come
to fight, they are not angry, they are
afraid; they are banging on my window
to be let in, terror in their faces, a deep
darkness like the heart of man, but
I refuse them entry. I know they
must look into darkness to find light,
that darkness comes to make us
see light. So I leave them
in London's cold darkness,
for humanity depends on them.

I return to my mattress to the delight of
the springs who noisily get back to their
unequal but envy-free work.

Mandela Stole my Freedom

My eyes were swollen shut—
purple-black, battered like bloody slabs
of uncooked steak had been placed
where my eyes once were—but I could see
the pain of the beast's punches.
My head was misshapen
after thirty five decades of punches;
flames enveloped my lungs,
concrete bags hung from my arms,
boulders strapped to my shoulders
bending my back like a banana.

A five-ton lead wrecking ball
rammed into my abdomen at every election;
I sang "we shall overcome" but doubted it
as the beast towered over me,
his fans egging him on to finish the fight,
my fans wiping tear gas from their eyes,
sitting in their prison cells.

But then the communist wall fell
and Ronald Reagan imposed sanctions
causing the colonial beast to stumble.
I managed to lift my fist,
draining the last life,
and flung it at the beast
and floored it. Five
six, seven, eight … it stirred
but lay flat on its back like a colossal statue
… nine, ten. It was over,
it was over, the fight was over,
we had overcome, I was free, I was free!

The boulders rolled away,
the wrecking ball floated into the air
like a child's balloon,
the concrete bags emptied.
My eyes opened for the first time
in centuries.
Free at last, free at last,
I was free at last!

But then that man spoke;
that man, Nelson Mandela, spoke:
"Our freedom is incomplete
without the freedom of the Palestinians,"
he said, and immediately
all the burdens returned,
three, four, five ...
and the beast was on his feet again
for my freedom fight to continue,
for the fight of the righteous to continue.

Hope

inspired by a Grant Cameron-Smith painting

Everything slides,
slips to bliss.

The bold tree
explodes into a sky
tumbling with pied crows
who flap and squawk
like Roman priests,
like black mothers
with white metal collars
singing blue notes
wrapped tightly with green
and red. Our land lays
barren but smiles broadly
in its promise of abundance
beyond the clouds.

There is peace
in this moment,
and then growth comes ...

... we all hold our breath
as everything slides,
slips to bliss
like memory
that rolls from yesterday
to hope.

The Blind That See—Version II

Abel is an old man who carries a gun;
he pretends to be blind,
walking erratically with his white stick
into oncoming traffic;
cars brake violently and swerve
to avoid crashing into this blind, old man.
His hope
is that some fool will stop to help him,
and then he'll take their cellphone, wallet, car,
and life, if they get in his way.

A cloud descends over me
as I watch with the morbidity
that we watch a lion attack a baby wildebeest,
or a policeman kick a woman unconscious,
or a child die of starvation
because we needed the money to have our nails done,
how someone stops.
A man in a suit, ironically,
the self-righteous type who seeks to do a good deed
to compensate for all the evil he does.
He runs into traffic to stop the oncoming cars,
takes the old man by the arm
leading him onto the sidewalk
and then,
into his car.
They drive off.
The cloud around me darkens.
I know what happens next.
Up ahead I see the car stop.
I hold my breath.
Daggers of lightning strike all around me,

thunder shakes the earth on which I stand,
I tighten my grip on my demons
as angry winds rip at my cheeks.
The suit gets out of the car, runs
around to the passenger door,
the old blind man appears,
arm in the suit's hand by the elbow,
and takes his place in the line to catch a bus.

I watch as he boards the bus when it comes,
other passengers helping. The suit waits
to ensure that Abel boards,
and then drives off.

Perhaps Abel really is blind!

The cloud lifts,
my demons go.
I wipe the tears from my cheeks
and my soul.

We Rise

Ambulance sirens scream
louder, more chaotic shrieks
than normal ... (normal?)
like they too have shock and anger
swirling in their shattered hearts.
They fade into weak wailing
cries of mourning mothers,
mothers of the fallen,
all our mothers.

And then empty silence ...
that we fill with silent embraces
just to feel closeness,
as if to remind our spirits
that humanity still exists
albeit tainted tonight.

In the cold darkness, love,
love smiles its warmness,
its hopeful light, love,
our gentlest healer,
our greatest need, our best response.

The fallen will rise,
with love,
we all will rise.

Boston, April 15, 2013
After the bombings at the Boston Marathon

Lightning Source UK Ltd.
Milton Keynes UK
UKOW02f0246010616

275346UK00001B/75/P